HIDDEN LANDMARKS OF BLACK HISTORY

Where are these girls? Turn to page 28 to find out.

BY JAY LESLIE

Children's Press®
An imprint of Scholastic Inc.

Special thanks to our consultant Deirdre Lynn Hollman, Senior Curriculum Specialist from the Black Education Research Center at Teachers College, Columbia University.

Library of Congress Cataloging-in-Publication Data available
978-1-5461-7785-2 (library binding) | 978-1-5461-7798-2 (paperback) | 978-1-5461-7875-0 (ebook)

10 9 8 7 6 5 4 3 2 1 26 27 28 29 30

Printed in China 62
First edition, 2026

Book design by Kathleen Petelinsek
Series produced by Spooky Cheetah Press

Photos ©: cover top center and throughout: The Telegraph (Macon, Ga.)/Tribune News Service/Getty Images; cover main: Hubbard & Mix/Library of Congress; cover background: SlamBang/Dreamstime; 1: Denver Public Library Special Collections, [ARL-178]; 4 top: Dom Slike/Alamy Images; 4 center: Bettmann Archive/Getty Images; 4 bottom: The Granger Collection; 5 top left: NPS/National Archives and Records Administration; 5 top right: Bill Manns/Shutterstock; 6 top: Sean Russell/Getty Images; 6 bottom: North Wind Picture Archives/Alamy Images; 7 top: North Wind Picture Archives/Alamy Images; 7 bottom left: The Picture Art Collection/Alamy Images; 8 top: IanDagnall Computing/Alamy Images; 9 top: Boston Athenaeum/Bridgeman Images; 9 center: Historic New England; 10 top: James Notman/Library of Congress; 11 top: Bettmann/Getty Images; 11 center: Elan Fleisher/Shutterstock; 11 bottom left: Maurice Savage/Alamy Images; 12 top: Pictorial Press Ltd/Alamy Images; 12 bottom: incamerastock/Alamy Images; 13: North Wind Picture Archives/Alamy Images; 14 top: Chris Hellier. All rights reserved 2025/Bridgeman Images; 14 bottom right: Rubens Alarcon/Alamy Images; 15 top: RLFE Pix/Alamy Images; 16 top: E. Sachse & Co./Library of Congress; 16 bottom: Currier & Ives/Library of Congress; 17 center: Universal History Archive/Universal Images Group/Getty Images; 17 bottom left: Glasshouse Images/Shutterstock; 18 top: State of North Carolina; 18 bottom: NPS/National Archives and Records Administration; 19 bottom right: Freedmen's Colony by Sonja Griffin Evans 2023; 20 top: H. Armstrong Roberts/Classicstock/Getty Images; 21 top: Wikimedia; 21 bottom right: Bettmann/Getty Images; 22 top: African American Museum & Library at Oakland/Oakland Public Library; 22 bottom: The Reading Room/Alamy Images; 23 top: Bill Manns/Shutterstock; 23 bottom: Craig Kohlruss/Fresno Bee/TNS/Alamy Images; 24 top: Craig Kohlruss/Fresno Bee/TNS/Alamy Images; 24 bottom: Gado/Getty Images; 25 top: George Sheldon/Alamy Images; 25 bottom right: Gary Kazanjian/AP Images; 26 top: Clark Brennan/Alamy Images; 26 center: Clark Brennan/Alamy Images; 26 bottom right: Pictorial Press Ltd/Alamy Images; 26 bottom left: Bettmann/Getty images; 27 top: Image courtesy of Aitina Fareed-Cooke; 27 center: Ron Howard/Popperfoto/Getty Images; 28 center right: Hustvedt/Wikimedia; 28 bottom: Denver Public Library Special Collections, [ARL-178]; 29 top right: Circa Images/Glasshouse Images/Alamy Images; 29 center: Everett Collection Historical/Alamy Images; 30 top: A.L. Lewis Museum; 30 bottom right: A.L. Lewis Museum; 31 center: Everett Collection Historical/Alamy Images; 31 bottom: National Park Service; 32 top: Our Oakland/Oakland Wiki; 32 bottom: Bev Grant/Getty Images; 33 top: DuSable Black History Museum and Education Center.

All other photos © Shutterstock.

Front cover: Students and teachers pose outside the Penn School in South Carolina.

TABLE OF CONTENTS

INTRODUCTION

When you think about important places in Black history, what comes to mind?

You might have heard of the Lincoln Memorial in **Washington, DC**. That is where Dr. Martin Luther King, Jr., gave his famous "I Have a Dream" speech. Or maybe you are familiar with **Montgomery, Alabama**. The bus **boycott** in that city led to the desegregation of public transportation. How about the **Woolworth's lunch counter in Greensboro, North Carolina**? That is where four college students staged a **sit-in**. They were **protesting** the rule that didn't allow them, or any other Black people, to eat there.

But there are probably many other important places in Black history that might be unknown to you—lesser-known sites that have also shaped the history of the United States. This book shines a spotlight on ten such places. These ten "hidden landmarks" include pioneering secret communities, inclusive vacation spots for African American families, groundbreaking musical sites, and more!

Learning about these places deepens our understanding of how Black Americans shaped the country we live in today. Celebrating these landmarks encourages us to value them. It allows us to expand our view of American history. Turn the page to discover the powerful stories behind these important places!

Where is this school and what happened there? Turn to page 18 to find out.

Have you ever heard of the buffalo soldiers? Turn to page 23 to learn more.

Turn to page 10 to read about a hidden stop on the Underground Railroad.

MAROON COMMUNITIES IN THE GREAT DISMAL SWAMP

A Safe Haven for Freedom Seekers

In the 1700s and 1800s, thousands of captive Africans escaped the Southern plantations where they were **enslaved** and forced to work. Many fled to a hidden place in North Carolina and Virginia called the **Great Dismal Swamp**.

The swamp was huge. It was also filled with thick brush, deadly snakes, and swarms of insects. These conditions made the swamp a difficult place to live. It also made the people living there hard to find. The Great Dismal Swamp became a refuge for **freedom seekers**. The people who lived there came to be known as **maroons**.

The Great Dismal Swamp used to cover one million acres. That is bigger than the state of Rhode Island.

Captive in the Colonies

In 1619, the first group of captive Africans was brought to Jamestown, in the colony of Virginia. They were forced to work for no pay for the people who lived there. It was the start of **slavery** in the area that would later become the United States. For more than 200 years, about 500,000 captive Africans were brought to the region.

Maroons built their homes on dry patches of land. They built communities where their children could be born free. These secret communities grew far from the reach of **slave-catchers**, who struggled to find their way through the swamp's dense wilderness.

After the **Civil War** began in 1861, some maroons felt they no longer needed to hide. Many joined the Union army. When the war ended in 1865, slavery became illegal in the United States. Many maroons who remained in the swamp left to start new lives in the open.

Uncovered!

Maroon colonies existed all over the Southern United States, the Caribbean, and Brazil.

AFRICAN MEETING HOUSE

Boston's First Black Church

In the early 1800s, slavery was illegal in Boston, Massachusetts. The Northern city became a destination for fugitives. Fugitives were enslaved people who had escaped the South. Yet free Black people in Boston still faced **discrimination**. For example, Black people were allowed to attend the same churches as white people. But when they did, they were treated poorly. Among other things, Black churchgoers had to sit in the worst seats. They could not vote on any church decisions.

A Church Built on Honor

Preacher Thomas Paul dreamed of a place where he and other Black Bostonians could worship freely—and be treated with respect. In 1806, Paul and twenty other people founded their own church. They called it the African Meeting House.

Danger in the North

Before the Civil War, slavery was illegal in Northern states. Many people who managed to escape enslavement fled to those states. But the Fugitive Slave Act of 1850 made even the North dangerous for freedom seekers. This harsh law required everyone to help catch escapees and return them to their enslavers. Anyone who refused could be fined or jailed.

The building served as the African Baptist Church of Boston. It also served as a school. Besides that, the African Meeting House was a gathering place for people who were determined to change the country for the better.

Interior

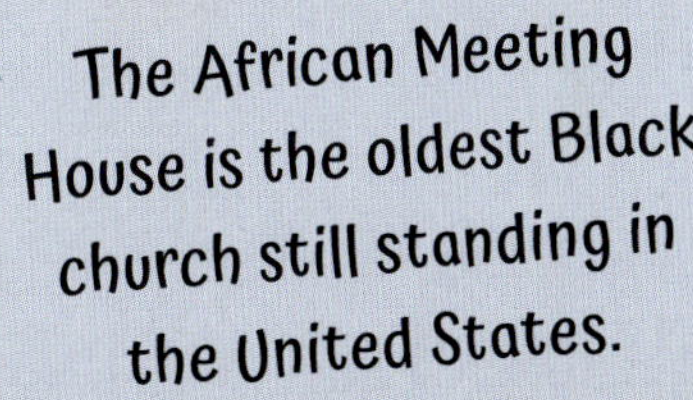

Uncovered!

In 1835, the Abiel Smith School opened next door to the African Meeting House. It was the first public school in the United States that was built specifically for Black children.

A Place for Change

In 1832, the African Meeting House became the center of the New England Anti-Slavery Society. Leading **abolitionists** gave speeches there. Abolitionists were people who fought to end slavery before the Civil War.

After passage of the Fugitive Slave Act of 1850, the African Meeting House became a stop on the **Underground Railroad**.

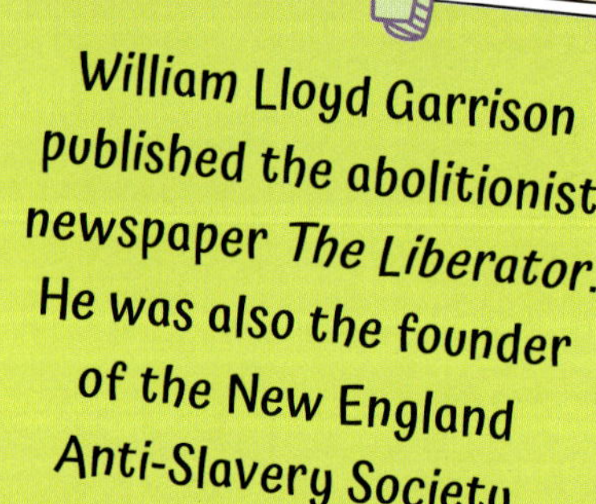

William Lloyd Garrison published the abolitionist newspaper The Liberator. He was also the founder of the New England Anti-Slavery Society.

Next Stop: Freedom

The Underground Railroad was not a real railroad with trains. It was a secret system of hidden paths and safe houses that enslaved people could use while escaping to freedom. People who guided the escapees to places where slavery was illegal were called **conductors**.

In 1861, tensions over slavery led to the Civil War. At first, Black men were not allowed to fight for the Union. That changed in 1862. One year later, in 1863, activist **Frederick Douglass** went to the African Meeting House to meet with Black men and encourage them to join the **Union army**.

Men of color to arms!

Today the African Meeting House is a National Historic Landmark that is owned by the **Museum of African American History**.

The 54th Regiment of the Massachusetts Volunteer Infantry was one of the first Black regiments of the Civil War.

CONGO SQUARE

A Meeting Place for Many Cultures

New Orleans in the early 1800s

For most of the 1700s, Louisiana was a French colony. In 1722, New Orleans became the capital. It was a city built on slavery. Captive Africans had to live by a set of rules called the **Code Noir**.

According to the Code Noir, neither enslaved people—nor anyone else—could work on Sunday. On their one day off, enslaved people gathered to socialize in public spaces all over the city.

Code Noir

King Louis XIV of France passed the Code Noir, or Black Code, in 1685. It was a set of laws to control enslaved Africans living in French colonies. The rules said that enslaved people had to convert to Catholicism, could not gather in large groups, and could be punished harshly if they tried to escape. Black Codes would continue to be used to control Black people throughout American history.

These gatherings continued—and even grew—after Louisiana became part of the United States. The mayor of New Orleans became uneasy. He made a new rule in 1817. From then on, all Black gatherings had to happen in one spot on the edge of the city. That spot became known as Congo Square.

People singing and dancing in Congo Square

In Congo Square, enslaved people from different West African cultures found joy and freedom of expression through community. They sang, danced, and played music using West African rhythms and melodies. These gatherings helped enslaved people keep their diverse traditions and languages alive. That was not easy to do under the harsh conditions of slavery. Celebrating their African **heritage** was an act of resistance.

Birthplace of Jazz

Congo Square became a place where people and music of all kinds mixed together. A new culture known as **Creole** was created. Different African dance styles, like the bamboula, calinda, congo, and juba, blended into something unique.

Local white leaders felt threatened by the crowds of enslaved people in Congo Square. They created even more rules to restrict the gatherings. Eventually, they turned Congo Square into a playground that only white people could use.

The bamboula is a dance set to the music of a bamboula drum.

Uncovered!

In 1893, white leaders in New Orleans renamed Congo Square after Confederate general P.G.T. Beauregard. The name Congo Square was not officially restored until 2011—more than one hundred years later.

CONGO SQUARE

Congo Square is in the "vicinity" of a spot which Houmas Indians used before the arrival of the French for celebrating their annual corn harvest and was considered sacred ground. The gathering of enslaved African vendors in Congo Square originated as early as the late 1740's during Louisiana's French colonial period and continued during the Spanish colonial era as one of the city's public markets. By 1803, Congo Square had become famous for the gatherings of enslaved Africans who drummed, danced, sang and traded on Sunday afternoons. By 1819, these gatherings numbered as many as 500 to 600 people. Among the most famous dances were the Bamboula, the Calinda and the Congo. These African cultural expressions gradually developed into Mardi Gras Indian traditions, the Second line and eventually New Orleans jazz and rhythm and blues.

CONGO SQUARE WAS LISTED ON THE NATIONAL REGISTER OF HISTORIC PLACES ON JANUARY 28, 1993.

Yet the African influence of Congo Square never faded. Some of the greatest jazz musicians, like **Jelly Roll Morton** and Louis Armstrong, grew up in New Orleans in the early 1900s. They were inspired by the musical traditions that had their roots in Congo Square. Morton and Armstrong took the rhythms and melodies from the square and turned them into early jazz music.

These musicians and others helped extend Congo Square's **legacy** far beyond New Orleans. As jazz musicians moved to cities like Chicago and New York, they carried the sounds of Congo Square with them.

Creole Culture in New Orleans

The Creole population in New Orleans is made up of people with cultural roots in France, Spain, African countries, and Caribbean islands. They brought together a mix of languages and created their own, called Louisiana Creole. Creole food is known for being spicy and flavorful, with African-inspired dishes like **gumbo**. That is a stew made from seafood, meat, and vegetables.

THE FREEDMEN'S COLONY ON ROANOKE ISLAND

A Free Town for Freed People

In 1862, during the Civil War, the Union captured **Confederate forts on Roanoke Island** in North Carolina, a state that was part of the Confederacy.

Union general Ambrose Burnside led the assault on Roanoke Island.

About two hundred enslaved people who had been forced to work in the forts were allowed to continue living there as **freedmen**. Soon enslaved people from nearby plantations fled to Roanoke Island to join the freedmen. In May 1863, the US government took over a portion of land on Roanoke Island. There, the formerly enslaved people could build their own lives in what became known as a freedmen's colony.

Uncovered!
The colony on Roanoke Island was one of about one hundred camps set up by the Union across the South for formerly enslaved people.

Freedmen in the Union Army

During the war, many enslaved people fled their enslavers for the protection of the Union army. Some men were able to become soldiers. Other men—and women—helped the Union army in other ways. They did physical work, such as cooking and cleaning. They also became scouts and spies. Their difficult, dangerous work helped the Union win the Civil War.

Growth and Struggles

Freedmen on Roanoke Island worked hard to create a new life. They built homes, **schools**, and a **church**. Teachers from the North came to help, offering classes for adults and children. For many formerly enslaved people, it was their first chance to learn how to read and write. This was an exciting time for people who had been denied an education for so long.

At its height, the colony's population reached almost four thousand. But as more people arrived, life on the island became difficult. The land wasn't good for farming, and not enough food could be grown to feed everyone. Overcrowding also led to the spread of disease.

Uncovered!
Many of the teachers on Roanoke Island came from New England.

End of an Era

After the Civil War ended in 1865, much of the property that had been taken from the Confederates was returned to its original owners. The people who had worked so hard to build the **freedmen's colony** on Roanoke Island were told to leave. By 1870, the population had dwindled from almost four thousand to just three hundred. Some **descendants** of those people still live on Roanoke Island, more than a century later.

Not Truly Free

Before the Civil War, small numbers of enslaved people were able to purchase their freedom and continue living in the South. They often worked as skilled laborers, and some even owned land. However, even though the people were free, they had to follow strict rules that limited their rights. Black people were not allowed to vote, serve on juries, or travel without permission in many places. They also had to carry **manumission** papers to prove they were free.

PENN CENTER

A School for Freedom and Change

During the Civil War, the Union captured St. Helena Island in South Carolina and freed the enslaved people who lived there. White abolitionists Laura Towne and Ellen Murray founded the Penn School in 1862 to teach the newly freed people how to read and write. This was the first school in the South created specifically for freedmen children. Many **Gullah Geechee children** attended the school.

Gullah Geechee People

The Gullah Geechee people are Black Americans who live in coastal areas called the Sea Islands, from North Carolina to Florida. Their **ancestors** were enslaved on plantations in this area. Their unique culture began during slavery. At that time, people from different African heritages were brought to the plantations and had to find ways to communicate. Over time, they blended their languages and customs, creating a new culture. The Gullah Geechee people speak a language called Gullah, which mixes English with African words. They are also known for their traditional crafts, such as **sweetgrass baskets**.

Charlotte Forten was the Penn Center's first African American educator. She joined Towne and Murray in 1862.

The Penn School was later known as the Penn Center. It was part of the Port Royal Experiment. That program provided education and land to formerly enslaved people. The school was named after William Penn, who was a member of the Society of Friends. That is a religious group of people who are also known as Quakers. One important aspect of the Quaker religion is a belief in the equality of all people.

In the 1950s and 1960s, the Penn Center played an important role in the **Civil Rights Movement**. It became a training center for activists. Leaders including **Dr. Martin Luther King, Jr.**, came to the Penn Center to plan and prepare for protests.

I have a dream that my four little children will one day live in a nation where they will not be judged by the color of their skin but by the content of their character.

Uncovered!
Dr. King composed his most famous speech, "I Have a Dream," while staying at the Penn Center.

ALLENSWORTH

California's First All-Black Town

In 1908, a new town appeared in California that was different from anything that had come before. Allensworth was the first town in the state to be entirely **founded, funded, and governed by African American people**.

The town was created by a group of men led by **Colonel Allen Allensworth**. Allensworth had been born into slavery in 1842. When he was young, he secretly learned to read. That was a skill forbidden to enslaved people. When Allensworth was caught, enslavers separated him from his mother as punishment.

Allensworth did not let this hardship stop him. In 1862, during the Civil War, he escaped enslavement by disguising himself as a Union soldier and marching off with a nearby regiment. He went on to serve in the Union navy and later served as a **chaplain** for the **buffalo soldiers**. By the time he retired in 1906, Allensworth had been promoted to lieutenant colonel. He was the first African American person to gain that rank and the highest-ranking Black officer in the US Army.

Buffalo Soldiers

After the Civil War, regiments of African American soldiers were formed to fight on the Western frontier. At the time, the US Army was fighting Native American tribes who lived on the Plains, such as the Apache, the Comanche, and the Cheyenne. Members of the 10th Cavalry were nicknamed buffalo soldiers by their Native American foes. Some say the name came from the soldiers' fierce fighting style. Soon soldiers from all the Black regiments took on the same nickname.

In 1908, after Allensworth had retired from the military, he and four other Black men decided to start a town where African Americans could live without **racism**. They bought eight hundred acres in California and built the town of Allensworth.

This is a photo of Allensworth in 2019.

A New Tuskegee

By 1910, the town of Allensworth had grown. It soon included important buildings like a schoolhouse, courthouse, hotel, Baptist church, and library. Residents also opened businesses, including general stores, a bakery, and a blacksmith shop.

The original Allensworth schoolhouse, which was built in 1912, is still standing.

Allensworth wanted his new town to become the **"Tuskegee of the West."** His goal was for the town to become self-sufficient. That means the residents could produce everything they needed to live independently. The town was on its way to achieving that goal, but problems eventually arose.

The Tuskegee Institute

The Tuskegee Institute was founded in Alabama in 1881 to help African Americans get a good education. Its founder, **Booker T. Washington**, believed that learning skills like farming, carpentry, and teaching would help Black people succeed. The school became famous for its focus on this type of practical training.

Access to clean water was unreliable, which made farming difficult. In 1914, the **Santa Fe Railway** no longer stopped in Allensworth, making it harder for residents to transport goods.

Later that year, Colonel Allensworth passed away, which left the town without its leader. And after World War I, economic difficulties forced many people to leave in search of better opportunities. This caused the town's population to decline.

By 1973, the town's population had dropped so much that Allensworth no longer appeared on maps. But the proud legacy of the town lives on. Today, it is **Colonel Allensworth State Historic Park**.

The park was established in 1974. Many of the town's original buildings can be seen there.

Uncovered!

Eatonville, Florida, is the oldest town in the United States completely established and run by Black people. It was founded in 1887.

THE COLORED MUSICIANS CLUB

A Place to Play and Learn

In the early twentieth century, the United States was segregated. **Segregation** was the practice of separating Black and white people, and having different rules for each group. Black people were forced to stay separate from white people in public places, including schools, restaurants, and theaters. Black musicians could not play at the same clubs as white musicians. They did not receive fair treatment, equal pay, or good working conditions, either.

COLORED ENTRANCE ONLY

COLORED MUST SIT IN BALCONY

These are signs that were used during segregation.

In 1918, a group of Black musicians opened their own space in the city of Buffalo, New York. It was called the Colored Musicians Club. The club became one of the few places where Black musicians could play, practice, and perform without worrying about being treated unfairly. It quickly gained fame for the popular musicians who performed there, like jazz legends **Count Basie** and **Ella Fitzgerald**.

The Colored Musicians Club (shown here in 2022) is the oldest African American-owned music club in the United States.

But the club was not just about big performers. It was also a place for learning. The musicians offered workshops and lessons so people in the community could learn to make music, too.

Today the Colored Musicians Club is still buzzing with life and bursting with music, keeping the Buffalo jazz scene in full swing.

Musicians on the Move

During segregation, Black musicians were often banned from playing for white audiences, and Black audiences were banned from many music halls. These restrictions led to the creation of the Chitlin' Circuit. That was a group of entertainment spots across the country that welcomed Black performers and audiences. This circuit, which included the Colored Musicians Club, was popular from the early 1900s through the 1960s. Many famous Black musicians, like James Brown and **Aretha Franklin**, started their careers on the Chitlin' Circuit.

Uncovered!

Because Black musicians were regularly denied service at restaurants, performers on the Chitlin' Circuit often traveled with their own canned food.

LINCOLN HILLS

A Mountain Sanctuary During Segregation

In the 1920s, African Americans who wanted to go on vacation did not have many options. Most resorts and parks in the United States were segregated. Black families were not welcome.

Two men from Colorado, E.C. Regnier and Robert Ewalt, wanted to create a place where African Americans could vacation without facing discrimination. So in 1922, they founded the mountain resort of Lincoln Hills in the Colorado Rockies.

Uncovered!
When it was founded, Lincoln Hills was the only Black resort west of the Mississippi River.

A huge inn called **Winks Lodge** was at the center of Lincoln Hills. Black Americans from all over the country came to relax and have fun there. In 1924, **Camp Nizhoni** became an important feature of Lincoln Hills. This summer camp for African American girls was all about learning, empowerment, and outdoor adventure.

The Great Migration

Between 1916 and 1970, millions of African Americans moved from the rural South to cities in the North and West. Life in the South was hard because of strict segregation laws and few job opportunities. But in cities like Denver, Colorado, which is located near Lincoln Hills, African Americans found work in factories and on railroads. Chicago, Detroit, and New York were also popular destinations. This movement helped spread African American culture across the country.

Lincoln Hills faced challenges during the Great Depression and World War II, but the biggest change came in the 1960s. After the **Civil Rights Act of 1964**, segregation ended. African Americans could finally visit other resorts. That meant fewer people needed Lincoln Hills. It officially closed in 1965. Today, the site is home to Lincoln Hills Cares, which organizes outdoor activities for young people and families in Colorado.

Turn to page 31 to learn more about the Civil Rights Act.

AMERICAN BEACH

A Beach Vacation for Black Americans

In 1935, Black people weren't just barred from vacation spots. They were often barred from local beaches, too. Florida's first Black millionaire, Abraham Lincoln Lewis, wanted to do something about that. He envisioned a beach paradise where Black families could vacation and even own property without facing racial discrimination.

Lewis bought 216 acres of land on Amelia Island, off the coast of Florida. He turned it into a resort called **American Beach**.

American Beach quickly became the place to be. Black families from all over the country could go there to enjoy the sun, sand, and surf. The beach also hosted massive events like music festivals and beauty pageants. Although most visitors were African American, the beach was open to everyone.

Uncovered!
Famous people like author Zora Neale Hurston and musician Ray Charles visited American Beach.

A Step toward Equality

During the Civil Rights Movement, people across the country fought to end segregation. Their hard work led the government to pass the Civil Rights Act of 1964. The law made it illegal to discriminate against people based on race, color, religion, gender, or national origin. After the law passed, it became illegal for employers to refuse to hire someone just because of their race. The law also banned segregation in public places such as swimming pools, libraries, and public schools.

Dorothy Height (center, with President Lyndon B. Johnson) was one of the most influential women of the Civil Rights Movement.

But after segregation ended, tourism at American Beach declined. On September 10, 1964, Hurricane Dora hit Amelia Island. It destroyed many of the homes and businesses of the Black people who still lived there. The community tried to rebuild. But the damage from the hurricane and the effects of desegregation were difficult to overcome. Many restaurants and resorts closed their doors.

Today, the beach is remembered through the **A.L. Lewis Museum**, which opened in 2014.

ST. AUGUSTINE'S EPISCOPAL CHURCH

The Start of the Free Breakfast Program

The Black Panthers were a group of civil rights activists. They were known for fighting against racial injustice. They also worked to improve Black people's everyday lives. In 1969, many African American families were struggling with poverty and hunger. In response, the Black Panthers launched a free breakfast program at **St. Augustine's Episcopal Church** in Oakland, California. Their goal was to make sure **children had a good breakfast** before heading to school.

On the first day, just eleven children came for a meal of eggs, cereal, meat, oranges, and chocolate milk. But word quickly spread. By the end of that first week, the program was feeding one hundred thirty-five children. By the end of the first year, they had served twenty thousand children.

Uncovered!

The Black Panthers also delivered free groceries to families in need. They helped people register to vote and provided free healthcare to their communities.

The success did not stop there. Between 1969 and 1971, the Black Panthers started thirty-six different **free breakfast programs** throughout the United States.

A sign from the Illinois chapter of the Black Panthers' free breakfast program

But by 1971, not everyone was happy about the program that had started at St. Augustine's Episcopal Church. The US government was suspicious of the Black Panthers' political activism. And government leaders saw that the Panthers' power in the community was growing. False stories were spread in an effort to shut the program down. Donations became harder to collect. By the mid-1970s, many of the Black Panthers' free breakfast locations had closed.

Although the program came to an end, it made a lasting impact.

The Most Important Meal of the Day

The US government had started its own free breakfast program, called the School Breakfast Program, in 1966. At that time, the program was available only in a few cities. Later, after the government forced the Black Panthers' breakfast program to close, the government's program was expanded across the country. Today, American schools serve more than fourteen million breakfasts every day.

MAP

You have learned about ten important places that shaped our nation, ten hidden landmarks of Black history. Now you can map them and connect them to some well-known places of Black history. And keep exploring. There are many more hidden landmarks waiting to be celebrated!

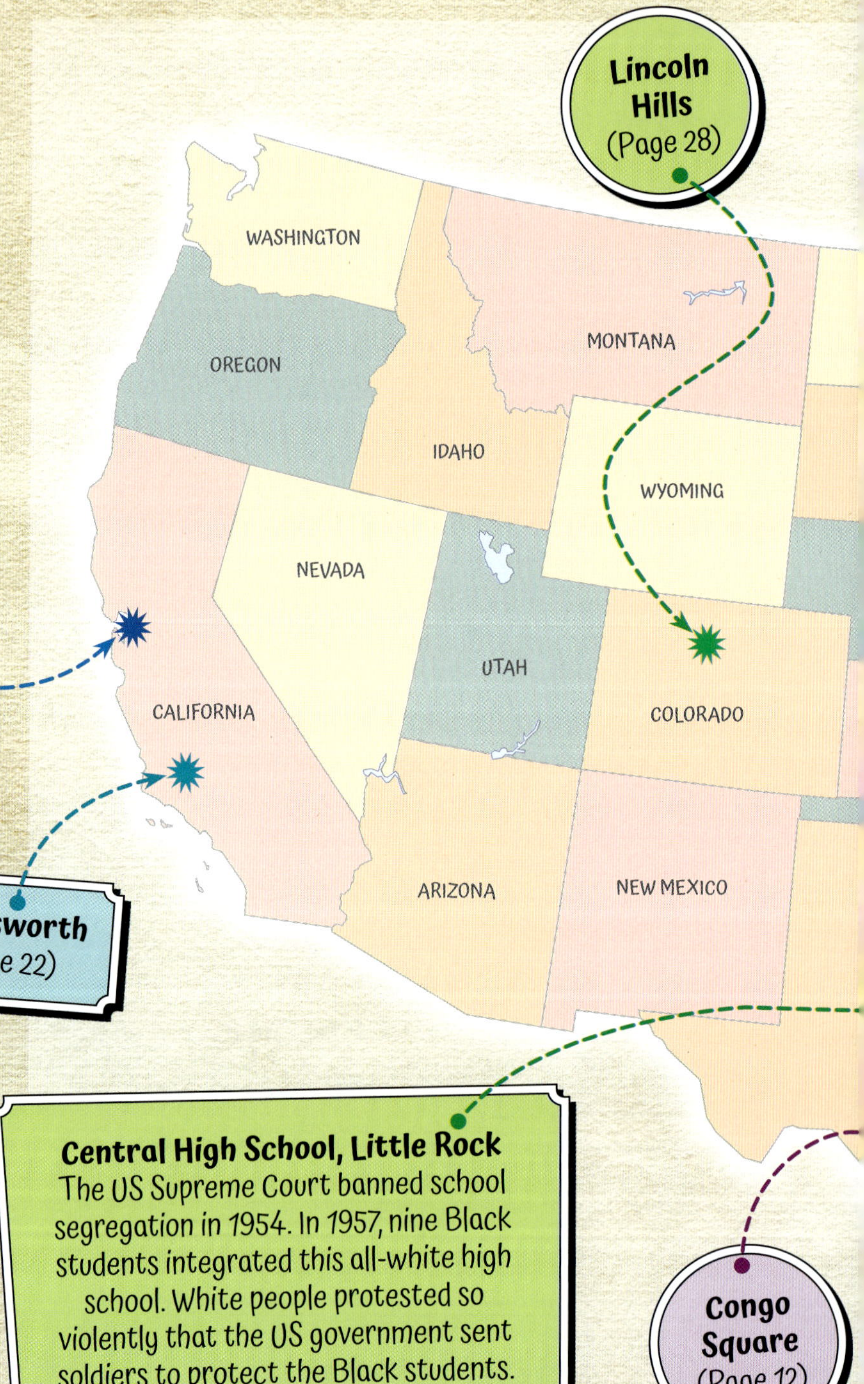

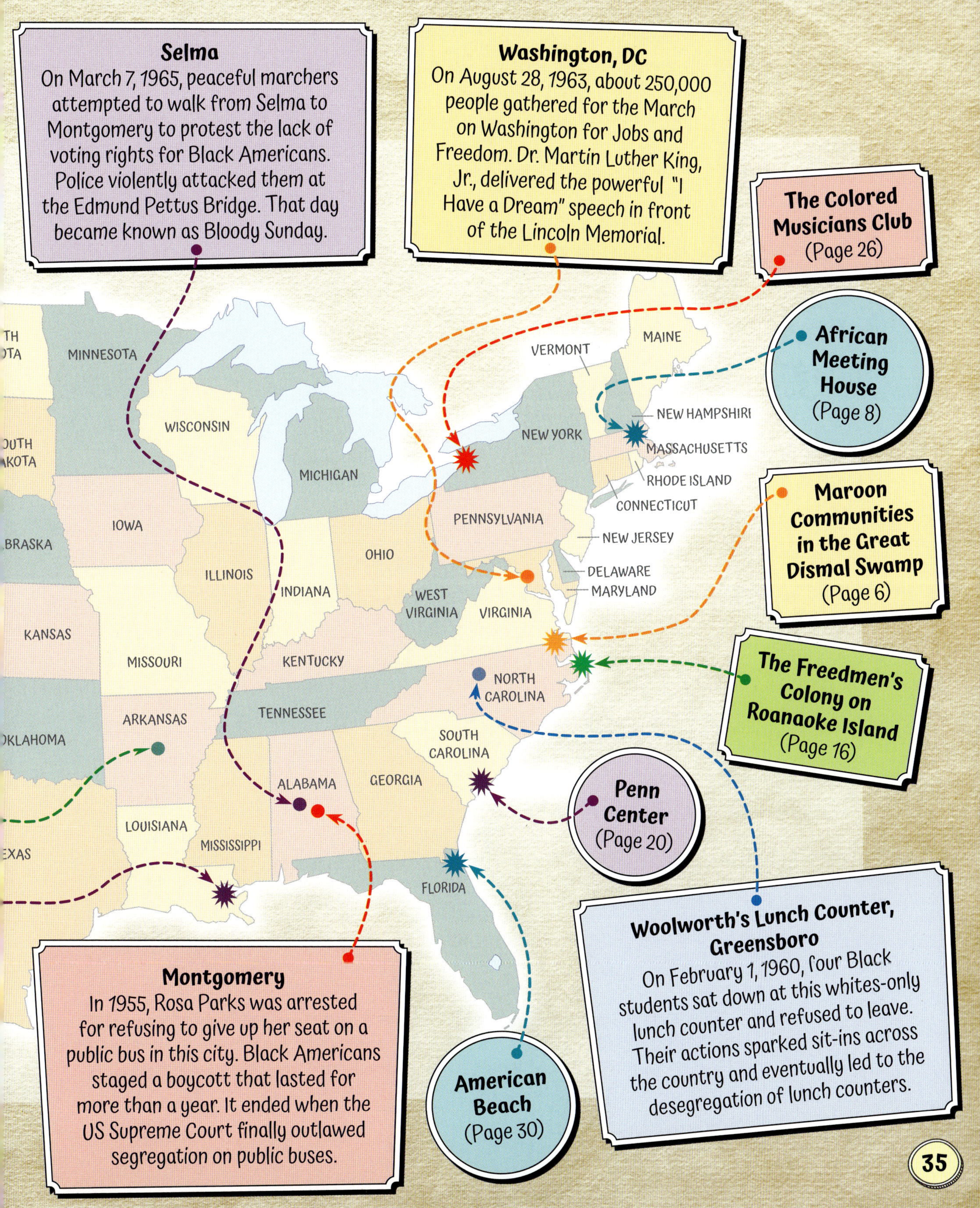
Selma
On March 7, 1965, peaceful marchers attempted to walk from Selma to Montgomery to protest the lack of voting rights for Black Americans. Police violently attacked them at the Edmund Pettus Bridge. That day became known as Bloody Sunday.
Washington, DC
On August 28, 1963, about 250,000 people gathered for the March on Washington for Jobs and Freedom. Dr. Martin Luther King, Jr., delivered the powerful "I Have a Dream" speech in front of the Lincoln Memorial.
The Colored Musicians Club
(Page 26)
African Meeting House
(Page 8)
Maroon Communities in the Great Dismal Swamp
(Page 6)
The Freedmen's Colony on Roanaoke Island
(Page 16)
Penn Center
(Page 20)
Woolworth's Lunch Counter, Greensboro
On February 1, 1960, four Black students sat down at this whites-only lunch counter and refused to leave. Their actions sparked sit-ins across the country and eventually led to the desegregation of lunch counters.
American Beach
(Page 30)
Montgomery
In 1955, Rosa Parks was arrested for refusing to give up her seat on a public bus in this city. Black Americans staged a boycott that lasted for more than a year. It ended when the US Supreme Court finally outlawed segregation on public buses.
MINNESOTA
WISCONSIN
MICHIGAN
IOWA
ILLINOIS
INDIANA
OHIO
PENNSYLVANIA
NEW YORK
VERMONT
MAINE
NEW HAMPSHIRE
MASSACHUSETTS
RHODE ISLAND
CONNECTICUT
NEW JERSEY
DELAWARE
MARYLAND
WEST VIRGINIA
VIRGINIA
KANSAS
MISSOURI
KENTUCKY
NORTH CAROLINA
TENNESSEE
ARKANSAS
SOUTH CAROLINA
ALABAMA
GEORGIA
LOUISIANA
MISSISSIPPI
FLORIDA

GLOSSARY

abolitionists (ab-uh-LISH-uh-nists) people who worked to end slavery before the Civil War

ancestors (AN-ses-turz) members of your family who lived long ago, usually before your grandparents

boycott (BOI-kaht) refusal to do business as a punishment or protest

chaplain (CHAP-lin) a priest, minister, or rabbi who works in the military, or in a school or prison

Civil Rights Movement (SIV-uhl RITES MOOV-muhnt) the fight for racial equality and citizenship in the United States that started in the mid-1950s and became famous for using nonviolent protests and civil disobedience to change unfair laws and practices

Civil War (SIV-uhl WOR) the war in the United States between the Confederacy, or Southern states, and the Union, or Northern states, which lasted from 1861 to 1865

Creole (KREE-ohl) a person of mixed French or Spanish and Black descent speaking a dialect of French or Spanish

descendants (di-SEN-duhnts) your descendants are your children, their children, and so on into the future

discrimination (dis-krim-i-NAY-shuhn) prejudice or unfair behavior to others based on differences in such things as age, race, or gender

enslaved (en-SLAYVD) held involuntarily and forced to work without pay under threat of violence or death

freedmen (FREED-men) people who were once enslaved but have been set free

freedom seekers (FREE-duhm SEE-kerz) people who are trying to escape from slavery to gain freedom

heritage (HER-i-tij) traditions and beliefs that countries, societies, or people consider an important part of their history

infantry (IN-fuhn-tree) the foot soldiers of an army

legacy (LEG-uh-see) something handed down from one generation to another

manumission (man-yuh-MISH-uhn) the act of an enslaved person becoming legally freed by the person who enslaved them

maroons (muh-ROONZ) people who escaped from enslavement and lived in a hidden community with others who had also escaped

protesting (PROH-tes-ting) taking part in demonstrations or statements against something

racism (RAY-si-zuhm) the unfair belief that one race is better than others, leading to mistreatment

regiments (REJ-uh-muhnts) military units

rural (ROOR-uhl) of or having to do with the countryside, country life, or farming

segregation (seg-ri-GAY-shuhn) the practice of separating Black and white people, and having different rules for each group

sit-in (SIT-in) a type of peaceful protest where people sit somewhere, like a restaurant, and refuse to leave until they are treated equally

slave-catchers (slayv-KACH-urz) people who were hired to find and return people who had escaped from enslavement

slavery (SLAY-vur-ee) the practice of holding people as property against their will, forcing them to work for no pay under threat of violence, and denying them the rights held by free persons

INDEX

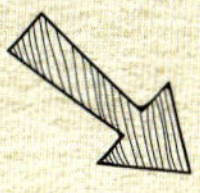

FURTHER READING

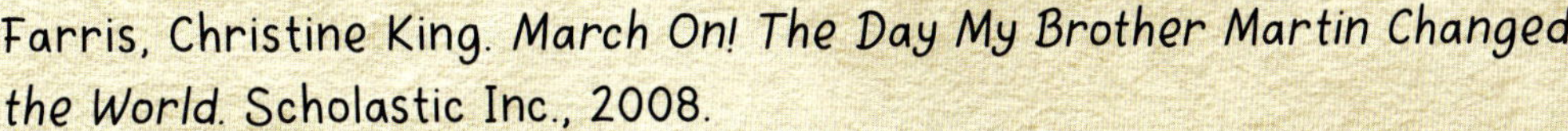

Farris, Christine King. *March On! The Day My Brother Martin Changed the World*. Scholastic Inc., 2008.

Grant, Kesha. *Women in the Civil Rights Movement* (A True Book). Scholastic Inc., 2020.

Hinton, KaaVonia. *The United States before the Civil War* (A True Book: Exploring the Civil War). Scholastic Inc., 2025.

McGhee, Jamie. *Reconstruction* (A True Book: Exploring the Civil War). Scholastic Inc., 2025.

Read the other books in this series:

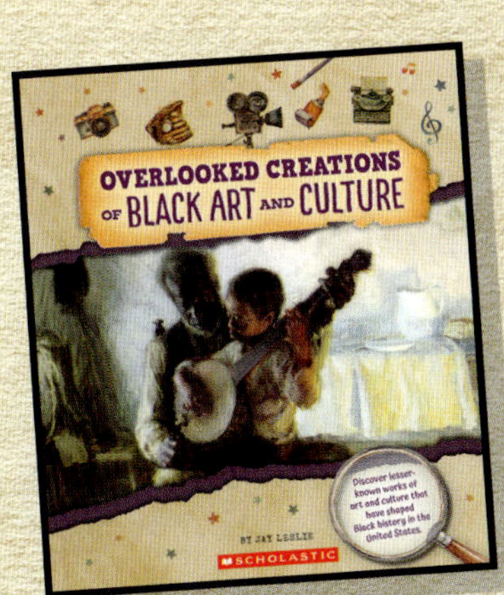

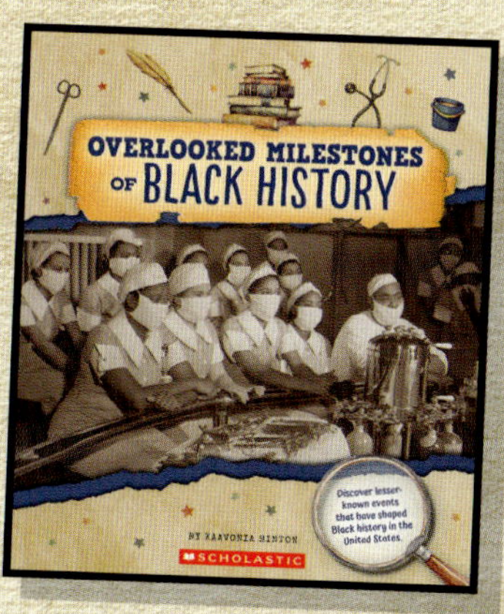

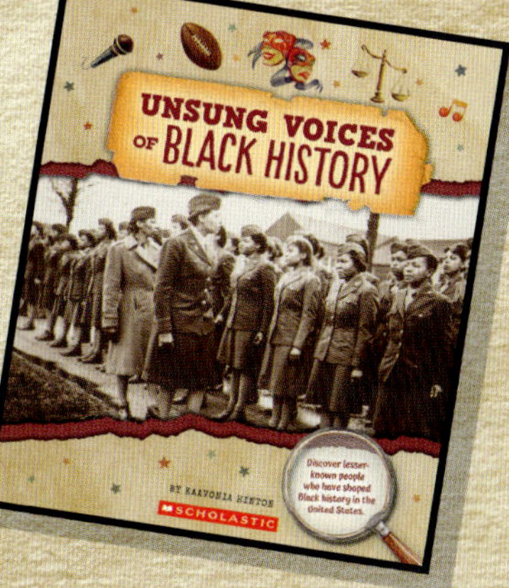

ABOUT THE AUTHOR

Jay Leslie has always loved to write. Everywhere she goes, she carries a notebook just in case she gets a new idea. Most of all, she loves to write the books that she wishes she'd had as a child.

Jay grew up in the United States, but now she lives in Germany, where she spends her time writing novels, learning new languages, and backpacking through the Schwarzwald. Say hi at jay-leslie.com.